Little Book of Patchwork

STARS

Chris Franses

David & Charles

Left: Four Ohio Star cushions – a simple block can be used to make a set of cushion fronts in different colourways

Opposite: A simple setting of nine blocks, a variation of the Friendship Star

A DAVID & CHARLES BOOK

First published in the UK in 2001

Text and designs
Copyright © Christine Franses 2001
Photography and layout
Copyright © David & Charles 2001

A catalogue record for this book is available from the British Library.

ISBN 0 7153 1085 2

Commissioning editor   Cheryl Brown
Text editor   Lin Clements
Book design   Ian Muggeridge
Photography   Stewart Batley

Printed in China by Leefung-Asco Printers Ltd. for David & Charles
Brunel House Newton Abbot Devon

CONTENTS

INTRODUCTION

There are nearly as many patchwork star patterns as stars in the sky. I have tried to choose a few representative examples of some the most familiar and to show you how to develop these patterns to make new ones. Some of the patterns are easy enough for absolute beginners, whereas others will provide a small challenge to those of you who have mastered the basic skills. I hope this book will encourage you to explore star patterns and to make some stunning and original quilts.

How to Use This Book

The book is one of a series and is intended to fit into your pocket or bag to accompany you on fabric-buying expeditions, rather than to be a comprehensive guide to all that is possible. Whilst not providing quilt patterns *per se*, the book features patterns for fifteen blocks. Each of these blocks is illustrated with a 4in block outline, different colourways and quilt settings. There is also a further selection of ten variations on these blocks.

Instructions are given for piecing each block and descriptions of a variety of different piecing methods are included. There are details on quilt construction, sashings, borders and bindings, plus a summary of quilting techniques. Instructions are also included to enable you to draft your own patterns and templates from the ones provided.

Yardage information (in both imperial and metric) is given with examples in the chapter, How Much Fabric?, to enable you to calculate how much fabric you need to buy. A minimum purchase of a fat quarter ($\frac{1}{2}$yd/0.5m of fabric cut in half to make two squares) is assumed and seam allowances are taken to be $\frac{1}{4}$in (rounded up to 1cm). The imperial and metric measurements given are not direct equivalents, only approximations; so decide which set of measurements you will use and stick to it throughout your project.

Opposite: A star sampler quilt, set with sashing, showing some of the blocks featured in the book.

STAR PATTERNS

Stars have inspired patterns in all cultures and periods of history from simple eight-pointed stars formed by printing a diamond repeat on African textiles to the five-pointed stars on Egyptian tomb paintings.

Stars are very easy geometric figures to draw, so it is no surprise to find they are popular patchwork designs. Star patterns can be based on the hexagon (or equilateral triangle) to make six-pointed stars, the octagon for simple eight-pointed stars, the square to create four- and eight-pointed stars, or the pentagon for five- and ten-pointed stars.

Stars are a frequent motif in Islamic design, and stars created on a hexagon grid form the basis of many Byzantine mosaics. Stars resembling the familiar traditional patchwork patterns can be found in Roman mosaics – six-pointed stars from equilateral triangles, simple eight-pointed stars, and more complex patterns based on triangles and squares resembling Ohio Star and Sawtooth Star.

The tiled floors of many of the great European churches and cathedrals frequently contain star patterns; some of these floors originate from medieval times, others are Victorian. A walk around many areas of Victorian housing will often reveal star patterns in tiled door steps and even in garden paths.

Try to record the tile patterns you find; some may already be familiar, but others offer a new slant on an old idea, and will no doubt inspire you to develop your own variation.

Opposite: A selection of antique quilts from the collection of Patricia Cox.

HOW MUCH FABRIC?

To work out how much fabric you need for a project you need to make several decisions first and then do a few sums. I hope the tables provided will take some of the complications out of the maths. The yardages given here tend to err on the generous side; once experienced in working out yardages you may be able to buy a little less than is suggested here. A fat quarter is a ½yd (0.5m) cut in two to give two 'squares' about 22 × 18in (56 × 50cm). The calculations which follow assume ¼in seams for imperial and 1cm seams for metric measurements. (Note that imperial and metric measurements in this section are not direct conversions, only equivalents.)

A word of caution before you slice your new fabric into millions of pieces: it really is advisable to make a sample block first, to ensure that the colours you have chosen work together. Sometimes they look great on paper, but in fabric something gets lost, especially using a patterned fabric. Don't despair if this is the case. Play around until you find a combination that *does* work.

Before you head for the shops however, there are a few questions you need to ask:

What overall size is your project to be?
From this you can decide on the size of the block and calculate the number of blocks required. Given below are average bed mattress sizes and the added extra to hang over the edge of the beds to make a suitably sized quilt. If the finished size of the quilt is crucial, measure your mattress to make sure, then add a suitable extra measurement to hang down the sides and foot, and to tuck under the pillow. *See Table opposite*

What size is the individual block to be?
First, look at the size of quilt you are making. To use 12in (30cm) blocks in a cot quilt may be tempting but they might be out of proportion; likewise 4in (10cm) blocks in a king size quilt would not be sensible so choose an individual block size that suits the project.

How many blocks are needed?
The number of blocks needed is calculated by multiplying the number of blocks across by the number of blocks down. These figures are worked out by dividing the quilt

measurements by the block size, as shown as follows.

Example:
A cot quilt needs:
72 (6 × 9) 4in (10cm) blocks or
24 (4 × 6) 6in (15cm) blocks.
A shorter cot quilt needs:
12 (3 × 4) 8in (20cm) blocks.
A longer cot quilt needs:
15 (3 × 5) 8in (20cm) blocks.
A double quilt needs:
80 (8 × 10) 10in (25cm) blocks or
72 (8 × 9) 10in (25cm) blocks or
56 (7 × 8) 12in (30cm) blocks.

Are you using sashing between blocks?
If you are using sashing then you will need fewer blocks for your quilt. One easy way to work this out is to draw the design including the sashing to scale on graph paper, then count up the number of blocks and measure the total width of the sashing.

How many pieces of each colour and shape are in each block?
You will need to work out the number of pieces of each colour and shape in each block and multiply this by the number of blocks in the quilt to arrive at the *total* number of each colour. This sounds more complicated than it is; with practise you will be able to 'guesstimate' quite accurately the amount of fabric you require for any number of blocks.

How much fabric do I need to buy?
Fabric used for patchwork is generally 44in (112cm) wide but check this, because if it is less you will probably need to buy more than I have indicated in the examples that follow.

	Mattress size	*Quilt size*
Cot	22 × 45in (55 × 115cm)	24 × 36in (60 × 90cm)
Single (twin)	36 × 72in (90 × 180cm)	60 × 92in (150 × 235cm)
Double	54 × 72in (135 × 180cm)	80 × 96in (205 × 245cm)
King	60 × 78in (150 × 200cm)	102 × 102in (260 × 260cm)

I have assumed that the easiest way to cut shapes from the fabric is to cut strips and slice the strips into the required shapes, which is fine for rotary cutting. If you prefer to draw around templates and then cut them out with scissors you may have a little more wastage and should allow for this in your shopping list.

For all shapes, to calculate the amount of fabric you need, work out how many of the shape will fit (with seam allowance included) across the width of the fabric. Then work out how wide a strip you will need for the width of the shape. Work out how many strips you need for the number of shapes to cut and multiply this by the width of the strips to give you the yardage. I have included some examples later on.

How many squares can be cut from specific lengths of fabric?
(Note that the cut lengths quoted below include seam allowances.) *See Table 1*

TABLE 1 - Squares		Fat quarter	½yd (0.5m)	¾yd (0.75m)	1yd (1m)
Cut size	*Finished size*	*Number*	*Number*	*Number*	*Number*
1½in (4.5cm)	1in (2.5cm)	168 (132)	348 (264)	522 (384)	696 (528)
2in (6cm)	1½in (4cm)	99 (72)	198 (144)	286 (216)	396 (288)
2½in (7cm)	2in (5cm)	56 (56)	119 (112)	170 (160)	238 (224)
3in (8cm)	2½in (6cm)	42 (42)	84 (84)	126 (126)	168 (168)
3½in (9.5cm)	3in (7.5cm)	30 (25)	60 (55)	84 (77)	120 (110)
4in (10cm)	3½in (8cm)	20 (20)	44 (40)	66 (60)	99 (90)
4½in (12cm)	4in (10cm)	16 (16)	36 (36)	54 (54)	72 (72)
5in (13cm)	4½in (11cm)	16 (16)	24 (24)	40 (40)	56 (56)
5½in (14cm)	5in (12cm)	9 (9)	21 (21)	28 (35)	42 (49)
6in (15cm)	5½in (13cm)	9 (9)	21 (21)	28 (28)	35 (42)
6½in (17cm)	6in (15cm)	9 (9)	12 (12)	24 (24)	30 (30)

How many right-angled, half-square triangles can be cut from specific lengths of fabric?

If you are rotary cutting, you can cut strips of the appropriate width, cut them into squares and then slice the squares in half. To calculate the seam allowance, and thus the width of strip or size of square, you should add ⅞in (3.5cm) to the finished size of the triangle. (Note, the numbers yielded in metric in Table 2 are more or less the same as the imperial.) *See Table 2*

How many quarter-square triangles can be cut from specific lengths of fabric?

Right-angled, quarter-square triangles are made by slicing a square into four across the diagonals. To calculate the seam allowance and thus the width of the strip or size of the square to cut, you need to add 1¼in (4.8cm) to the finished size of the triangle. *See Table 3 page 12*

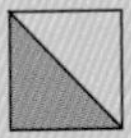

TABLE 2 - Right-angled, half-square triangles		Fat quarter	½yd (0.5m)	¾yd (0.75m)	1yd (1m)
Cut size	*Finished size*	*Number*	*Number*	*Number*	*Number*
1⅞in (6cm)	1in (2.5cm)	108	396	572	792
2⅜in (7.5cm)	1½in (4cm)	98	238	340	476
2⅞in (8.5cm)	2in (5cm)	72	168	252	336
3⅜in (9.5cm)	2½in (6cm)	50	120	168	240
3⅞in (11cm)	3in (7.5cm)	32	88	132	198
4⅜in (12.5cm)	3½in (9cm)	32	72	108	144
4⅞in (13.5cm)	4in (10cm)	18	48	80	112
5⅜in (15cm)	4½in (11.5cm)	18	48	64	96
5⅞in (16cm)	5in (12.5cm)	18	42	56	84
6⅜in (17.5cm)	5½in (14cm)	18	24	48	60
6⅞in (18.5cm)	6in (15cm)	18	24	36	60

How many 45° diamonds can be cut from specific lengths of fabric?

The diamonds used in eight-pointed stars are 45° diamonds and can be cut from strips of fabric. First, measure the width of the diamond and add a seam allowance of ¼in (1cm) to both sides to give the width of strip to cut. Now measure the length of the diamond and add ¾in (3cm) to this measurement for the length of the diamond to cut, and to work out how many will fit across the width of the fabric. *See Table 4*

How many equilateral triangles can be cut from specific lengths of fabric?

Six-pointed stars are made from equilateral triangles (with 60° angles), and these also occur in some blocks such as 54-40 or Fight. Again, to work out how many can be cut from a strip of fabric you need to add ⅞in (3.5cm) to the finished length to get the cut length and ¾in (3cm) to the height to get the width of the strip. (Note, the numbers yielded are practically the same in imperial and metric.) *See Table 5*

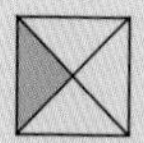

TABLE 3 - Quarter-square triangles

		Fat quarter	½yd (0.5m)	¾yd (0.75m)	1yd (1m)
Cut size	*Finished size*	*Number*	*Number*	*Number*	*Number*
2¼in (7.3cm)	1in (2.5cm)	324 (168)	608 (360)	836 (600)	1140 (780)
2¾in (8.8cm)	1½in (4cm)	168 (120)	384 (240)	576 (384)	832 (528)
3¼in (9.8cm)	2in (5cm)	120 (100)	260 (220)	416 (308)	572 (440)
3¾in (10.8cm)	2½in (6cm)	80 (80)	176 (160)	308 (240)	396 (360)
4¼in (12.3cm)	3in (7.5cm)	80 (64)	160 (144)	240 (216)	320 (288)
4¾in (13.8cm)	3½in (9cm)	48 (48)	108 (96)	180 (160)	252 (224)
5¼in (14.8cm)	4in (10cm)	48 (36)	96 (84)	160 (140)	192 (168)
5¾in (16.3cm)	4½in (11.5cm)	36 (36)	84 (72)	112 (96)	168 (144)
6¼in (17.3cm)	5in (12.5cm)	24 (24)	56 (48)	112 (96)	140 (120)
6¾in (18.8cm)	5½in (14cm)	24 (16)	48 (40)	72 (60)	120 (100)
7¼in (19.8cm)	6in (15cm)	24 (16)	48 (40)	72 (60)	98 (80)

Table 4 - 45° diamonds

Block size	Fat quarter Number	½yd (0.5m) Number	¾yd (0.75m) Number	1yd (1m) Number
4in (10cm)	108	216	329	432
6in (15cm)	60	130	195	260
8in (20cm)	40	88	132	176
9in (22.5cm)	32	77	110	154
10in (25cm)	28	70	100	140
12in (30cm)	24	54	81	108

Table 5 - Equilateral triangles

Cut size	Finished size	Fat quarter Number	½yd (0.5m) Number	¾yd (0.75m) Number	1yd (1m) Number
1⅞in (6cm)	1in (2.5cm)	153	324	468	648
2⅜in (7.5cm)	1½in (4cm)	91	266	280	392
2⅞in (8.5cm)	2in (5cm)	72	156	234	312
3⅜in (9.5cm)	2½in (6cm)	50	110	176	242
3⅞in (11cm)	3in (7.5cm)	36	76	133	171
4⅜in (12.5cm)	3½in (9cm)	28	64	96	128
4⅞in (13.5cm)	4in (10cm)	21	45	75	105
5⅜in (14.5cm)	4½in (11.5cm)	18	42	70	84
5⅞in (15.5cm)	5in (12.5cm)	18	39	52	78
6⅜in (16.5cm)	5½in (13.5cm)	10	24	48	60
6⅞in (18.5cm)	6in (15cm)	10	22	44	55

Worked Example 1 – Single Bed Quilt

(Imperial measurements)

Overall Size: 52 × 80in (including sashing and border).

Quilt Pattern: Pieced star.

Block Size: 12in blocks, with 2in wide sashing between blocks and 4in wide border, which means I need 3 blocks across (3 × 12in = 36in) and 5 blocks down (5 × 12in = 60in) *(see plan opposite)*.

Calculations: First I work out how many of each colour piece I need, as follows:

• There are 15 blocks (5 × 3)in this quilt, each composed of half-square triangles, 16 of each colour in each block. I therefore need 15 × 16 blue triangles and 15 × 16 white triangles, that is, 240 of each.

• The block size is 12in, the block is a four-patch, the triangles are therefore 3in half-square finished size. I need to cut squares 3⅞in for each pair of triangles. From Table 2, I see I can cut 198 from 1yd of fabric and 32 from a fat quarter, I would therefore need to buy 1½yd each of blue and white for the triangles.

• The sashing strips are white, 2in by 12in finished size, so I need to cut them 2½in by 12½in. I can cut three long strips each 12½in from one width of fabric, so I need to cut thirteen strips to ensure I have the 38 I need (i.e. 13 × 2½in (the width of the strips) = 32in, or 1yd of fabric).

• The sashing squares are blue, 2in finished size (2½in cut size) and I need 24; I can cut these from a fat quarter according to Table 1 on page 10.

• The border strips used in this single quilt are also blue. If I don't mind joining these strips then I can cut eight strips 4½in wide across the width of the fabric – two for each border – which makes 36in or 1yd, plus a bit for luck. If I don't want to join the border strips but prefer to cut them from one length of fabric then I will need to buy at least 82in to cut the two longer borders; say 2½yd.

• So my fabric shopping list will read:

White fabric = 1½yd for triangles plus 1yd for sashing strips, plus a bit for 'in case' = 2¾yd or even 3yd.

Blue fabric = 1½yd for triangles, ¼yd for sashing squares, and either 1yd or 2½yd for borders. I have decided not to join the borders, so I could cut the sashing squares from the fabric left over after I have cut the borders, but I will also need enough to cut bindings (another four strips 82in long × 2½in wide). So I need to buy 2½yd plus 1½yd plus ¼yd = 4¼yd (minimum).

Backing fabric = if using 90in wide, I will need 54in, i.e. 1½yd. If using 44in wide I will need two lengths joined down centre = 3yd.

Wadding (batting) = it's best to buy single bed size, checking the measurements given on the bag.

Worked Example 2 – Christmas Wall Hanging
(Metric measurements)

Overall Size: 70cm square, including a border all round 5cm wide.

Quilt Pattern: Eight-pointed star block.

Block Size: 20cm blocks. I need 9 blocks altogether for my design. (3 × 20cm across and 3 × 20cm down). I am using two different reds, one green and one white print (*see plan opposite*).

Calculations: I need to work out how many of each colour piece I need:

• I need to cut 24 dark red diamonds, 8 light red diamonds and 32 green diamonds. Each of these can be cut from a fat quarter of fabric, according to Table 4 on page 13.

• I also need 12 light red squares and 24 white ones; again these can be cut from a fat quarter (they are approximately 6cm finished size).

• To finish I need 8 green and 28 white quarter-square triangles 8.5cm finished size. The green ones can be cut from a fat quarter and the white ones from 75cm.

• The light red border needs two 5cm by 60cm strips and two 5cm by 70cm strips; if I don't want a join in the borders I need to cut four strips 7cm wide = 28cm fabric, plus a bit to allow for error.

• So my fabric shopping list will read:

Dark red = fat quarter.

Green = 2 fat quarters or 50cm.

White = 75cm.

Light red = 1m plus a bit for binding, if I decide to use this colour.

Backing and wadding (batting) = 1m each.

TECHNIQUES

This section contains information on basic patchworking techniques. There are several basic types of star block that require a similar construction method and these are detailed in this chapter, with an indication of the best method given with each block outline. The section is illustrated with figures and where necessary for clarity, some are marked WS (wrong side) and RS (right side) or R (reversed).

Using the Block Templates

The fifteen blocks featured in this book each have a 4in block outline provided, to be used as a basis for your patterns and templates. If you want a larger size block, or a metric block, the patterns are very easy to draw using the appropriate graph paper. For variations of the Eight-pointed Lemoyne Star you will need to use isometric graph paper – one that has a grid of diamonds, not squares.

Try to choose a size of block that does not complicate the maths – for instance a nine-patch block will be easier to work out if the final measurement is easily divided by three, e.g. 12in (30cm) or 15in (45cm), not 10in (25cm). Of course, you can always enlarge the templates given on a photocopier, but be aware that photocopying can distort very slightly, so your accurate block may not be quite so accurate afterwards – check it before sewing.

The outline blocks can also be used as colouring diagrams. Cover the block outline with tracing paper, or photocopy it several times, and use crayons or coloured pencils to try out different colourways for the block before cutting into fabric. Draw several blocks together – at least nine – and use this outline in the same way to judge how your colour scheme works as a quilt. Colour in the block in your chosen colours, then using this drawing as a guide, choose and cut your fabrics. If two adjacent triangles are the same colour, you may of course be able to cut them as one piece – why make extra work for yourself! You may also find it helpful to make a trial block using your chosen fabrics before cutting out an entire quilt. This ensures that the block size you have chosen looks good, that the templates are the right size, and that the fabrics look as good as you expected when put together. If the trial block is fine then use it in the quilt and carry on cutting out pieces, otherwise, think again, work out what is wrong with the block and, if necessary, use the trial one as a cushion or tote bag front.

MAKING TEMPLATES

The cheapest material for making templates is card, such as that from cereal boxes. Trace your pattern pieces onto tracing paper, glue this onto card and carefully cut out the shape. You can also mark the grain lines on templates where appropriate. The main drawback of card templates is that the more you draw round them, the more you wear them away, which will alter the shape and size gradually – something you may not notice until you try to join the first triangle you cut out to the last one. Special transparent template plastic can be bought from quilting suppliers and is an ideal, long-lasting solution. It is placed over the patterns to be traced and the shapes drawn with pencil before cutting out. It is also useful for cutting out from motif fabric as you can see exactly where the motif will finish up.

Remember always to label your templates. Another good idea is to keep the templates for a particular block, or set of blocks, in a small plastic bag, together with the instructions for making the block.

Make and cut out your templates carefully as any inaccuracy here will multiply severalfold as you make the quilt. Templates can be made with or without a seam allowance. For machine piecing, add the seam allowance to each template – mark on the template what size of allowance you have used (¼in or 1cm) – and use the raw edge of the fabric against the appropriate mark on the sewing machine guidelines to ensure an accurate match and seam; the lines you draw around these templates are the cutting lines.

For hand piecing, cut the templates without a seam allowance and 'guesstimate' the allowance when you cut out the pieces. The lines you have drawn around these templates become the sewing lines that you use as a guide for accurate matching of pieces. Mark your fabrics on the wrong side of the fabric with a soft pencil – remember the straight grain of the fabric needs to be along one edge, and preferably the outside edges of the block. Use as fine a line as possible as you are marking the seam line – a thick line will not only increase the chance of inaccuracies but will also show after sewing.

CUTTING THE FABRIC

Take care when cutting out your fabric that you leave a seam allowance if you need to – don't confuse hand-piecing and machine-piecing templates. For special effects use a transparent plastic template or make a window template from card (a template with the centre cut out and just the seam allowance or a bit extra left around the edge). These can be used to position the template exactly over a particular motif or over a section of pattern in a fabric to create a kaleidoscope effect where several pieces meet in the middle of a block – see the Evening Star block page 86. Use sharp fabric scissors to cut out the pieces for your block and take care with templates that are not symmetrical – it is wise to mark them so that you know which side to place down on the fabric; there is nothing more infuriating than discovering you have cut several mirror image pieces that will only fit in the block if you use the wrong side of the fabric. Seams are usually pressed to one side (towards the darker fabric) as pressing the seam open can make quilting more difficult.

PIECING THE BLOCKS

Piecing is the sewing together of the patches to make up the patchwork or block. It can be done by hand or machine; patches may also be sewn with a paper foundation either directly onto the paper, or pieced over the papers.

To ensure that you sew the block together in the right order and don't muddle pieces it is best, especially with more complex blocks, to first lay all the pieces out in the correct pattern on a cork or polystyrene tile. Each pair of pieces to be sewn can be picked up, stitched by your chosen method, and replaced on the tile in turn.

Hand Piecing over Papers

This method of hand piecing is sometimes referred to as English piecing. It allows very accurate piecing of small or intricate shapes and is particularly useful for shapes such as hexagons or diamonds where 'set in' pieces or Y seams occur (Fig 1). The Lemoyne Star and other eight-pointed star variations are examples of these.

Use the templates to cut out paper shapes without a seam allowance. Use a fairly stiff paper such as glossy magazines, or freezer paper – a wax-coated paper available in the United States for wrapping freezer items. An alternative is the wax-coated paper sometimes used to wrap photocopy paper, but be careful the print does not iron off onto the fabric.

Place these papers on the wrong sides of the fabric, fold over the seam allowance and

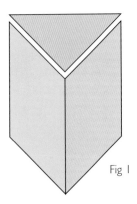

Fig 1

Hand Piecing without Papers

Following the piecing sequence, place two patches right sides together. Pin the seam lines at the corners, then pin the rest of the seam. Keep the pins at right angles to your seam line and keep checking that seam lines match and line up.

Knot your thread, remove the corner pin and insert the needle. Check that it has gone through both corners. Stitch along the seam line with a small running stitch adding an occasional back stitch for extra strength – this is known as 'piecing stitch'. Finish off with two or three back stitches and/or a knot. Press the seams towards the darker fabric. Continue to join patches together, following the piecing sequence, until the block is complete.

Machine Piecing

Cut out your pieces with an accurate and exact seam allowance – usually ¼in (or 1cm). No seam line is required for machine stitching, so pieces can be cut either with a rotary cutter or using templates. There are a great many books about rotary cutting, some of which are listed in the bibliography. Make machine piecing templates with a ¼in (or 1cm) seam allowance, then when you draw around the templates – in pencil on the

tack (baste) the fabric and paper together if using glossy paper, or iron the freezer paper in place and press the seam allowance over.

Place two pieces right sides together and oversew along the seam, taking care not to catch the paper in the stitches. Start stitching a little way from the corner, stitch back to the corner then along to the end. To finish, stitch back a little way and fasten off. This will reinforce the corners where wear always occurs first. You can start and finish your seams with either a backstitch or a knot, whichever method suits you best. The papers will be removed when all the patches are stitched together or the quilt top is complete.

wrong side of the fabric – the line you are drawing is the cutting line.

Place the first two pieces right sides together, matching the raw edges. Stitch, using a fairly long stitch (10 or 12 to the inch), from one edge to the other. Don't bother about fastening threads as you will stitch over these ends later, which will hold them firm.

If you have a great many similar pieces to join, just keep feeding them through the machine one after another without cutting the threads – you can do this later. For reasons that will be obvious once you've done it, this is known as chain-piecing.

Press the seams to one side, preferably to the darker fabric. When you come to join patches together these seams should butt up against each other making it easier to match seams. When you have several seams meeting at one point – the centre of eight-pointed stars for example – use pins to hold the pieces in position as you stitch. If the seams still slip while you are stitching, try placing a slip of paper on top of the seam; the presser foot will then push on the paper instead of the fabric, and help to keep the seams together and all the points neatly matching. The paper can easily be torn away afterwards, leaving neatly matched seams.

If, when you come to join rows of pieces together, you find that one is longer than the other, place the long one on the bottom and the shorter one on top (if possible) to take advantage of the fact that the feed dogs tend to gather and the foot tends to push and stretch the fabric. Likewise try to put a bias seam underneath and the straight one on top.

TYPES OF STAR PATTERN

Blocks are generally pieced in stages; practise looking at blocks and deciding the best piecing sequence for them. Most of the blocks in this book fall into one or more of the following categories – nine-patch, four-patch, eight-pointed star, or partial seam. Nine-patch and four-patch blocks, as implied, are made from nine or four units, or multiples thereof, which have been subdivided to make the star pattern.

Constructing Nine-patch Stars

These include Ohio Star, Friendship Star and 54-40 or Fight. Follow the coloured drawing you have made of your block and sew the individual pieces to complete the nine unit squares. The nine small squares can be sewn into pairs, and then threes to complete the rows of the block. Lastly, sew the three rows together to complete the block (see Figs 2a–2h on pages 23 and 24).

Constructing Nine-patch Stars

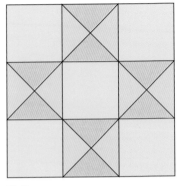

Fig 2a

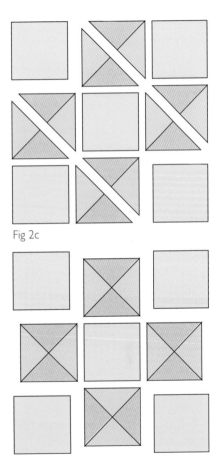

Fig 2c

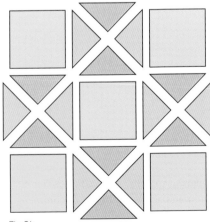

Fig 2b

Fig 2d

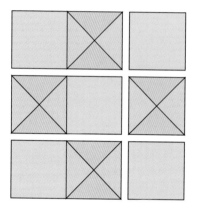

Fig 2e

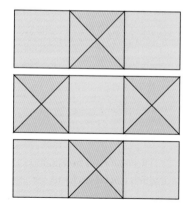

Fig 2f

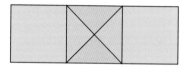

Fig 2g

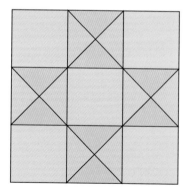

Fig 2h

Constructing Four-patch Stars

These include Indian Star and Simple Star, and are all subdivided into four or sixteen smaller square or rectangular units (Fig 3a). These stars are pieced in much the same way as nine-patch stars. The smaller units are pieced first and can then be joined into rows and the rows into blocks. Piece the central square and the corner squares (if necessary), then piece the star rectangles (Fig 3b).

Constructing Four-patch Stars

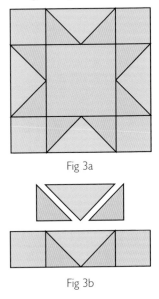

Fig 3a

Fig 3b

Blazing Star is also a four-patch block. Note from Fig 4a on page 26 that the block includes pieces that are mirror images of each other. One template can be used but must be *reversed* to cut the mirror image piece. If you wish, this block can be pieced over papers (see page 20) for greater accuracy. Remember to reverse the templates when cutting all the pieces AR, BR and CR (where R on the figures stands for 'reversed'). Follow Figs 4a–4d on page 26 for the piecing sequence.

Other four-patch blocks, including Interlaced Star, are subdivided diagonally across the block (Figs 5a–5d) on page 27. Some blocks, such as Skyrocket, are a slight variation on this theme. They are a conventional nine-patch or four-patch block on point in the centre with pieced triangles sewn to the four sides. Piece the centre block as a conventional block. Piece the corner triangles and then sew these to the four sides to complete the block.

Constructing Eight-pointed Stars

These are based on an octagon and examples include Lemoyne Star, Empire Star and Star of the East. These blocks often include a set-in or Y seam which can be tricky to sew, especially on the machine. First, sew the diamonds together into pairs, then the pairs into fours. Do not sew right to the edge of the fabric,

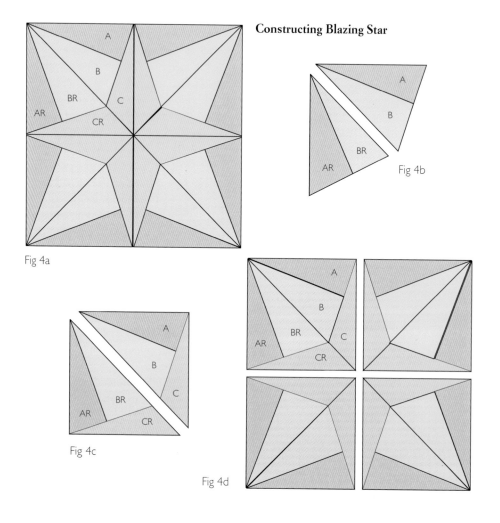

Constructing Blazing Star

Fig 4a

Fig 4b

Fig 4c

Fig 4d

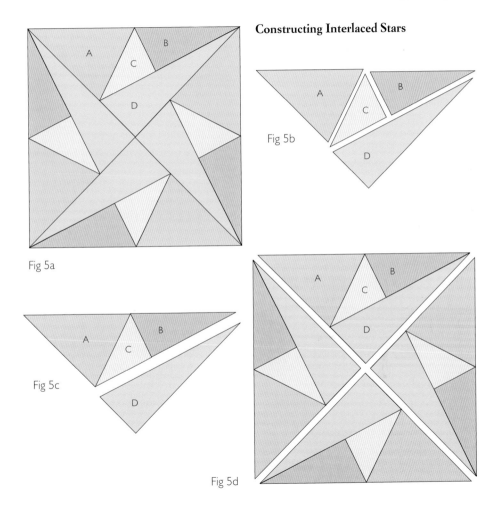

Constructing Interlaced Stars

Fig 5a

Fig 5b

Fig 5c

Fig 5d

stop at the end of the seam, even when machine piecing. Finally sew the two halves together to complete the star and press the seams – where all the seams meet at the centre press the seam allowances in a 'swirl'.

For the 'set in' pieces – the squares and triangles – I find it easier to do the triangles first, but everyone has their preference. Pin the first triangle in place, starting at the point where it joins the inside of the star. Stitch the first seam from the centre out. Then stitch the second seam, from the centre out. Repeat this for all four triangles. Pin one of the squares in place, again from the inside to the outer edge. Stitch in the same way: start at the inside and stitch out towards the edge. There may be a slight hole where the seam allowances meet. This is quite normal and will not show. If the corners are puckered then the seam allowances have not quite come together properly and a little unpicking and re-sewing may be needed.

An alternative to piecing the background is to appliqué the star onto a square of background fabric. Turn under the seam allowances, tack the star in place and carefully stitch round the star with a matching thread, using an invisible hemming stitch and ensuring that the star points are securely stitched.

An eight-pointed star block can also be pieced over papers – follow the instructions for hand piecing over papers on page 20. Adding the set-in triangles and squares is much easier and often more accurate by this method. The piecing sequence is exactly the same as sewing without papers – stitch the diamonds into pairs, then fours and finally complete the star. Then add the set-in triangles and squares to complete the block. The papers should be left in place until the quilt top is complete.

Constructing a Star with a Partial Seam

Some blocks require piecing in a certain sequence that needs a partial seam to be sewn before the block can be completed. Three examples of this type of construction are included in the book – Spinning Stars, Twisted Star and Eccentric Star. They all have a central shape – a square, octagon or pieced square – with the remaining parts of the block rotating round it.

Piece the outer parts of the stars first: for Spinning Stars sew the four main rectangles that encircle the central square; for Twisted Star sew a star triangle to each background triangle and to each background square; for Eccentric Star piece the central square and the four star rectangles that surround it.

Then for all stars with a partial seam take the first piece to be sewn around the central shape and sew less than halfway along the seam, then finish the stitching securely and finger press the seam. Now take the second piece, place it in position and stitch right along the length of the seam.

Continue to add pieces around the central shape until they are all stitched in place. Return to the unfinished seam and complete it. You may find it easier to start a little way beyond where you finished the seam, leaving a small gap; as long as the stitching is secured this will not matter – it's better than having a wrinkle. If you still have problems machining this partial seam, especially on small blocks, cut your losses and hand sew it.

JOINING BLOCKS INTO QUILTS

Many star quilts have sashing strips that separate the blocks, and most usually have borders; both sashing and borders can also be pieced. Blocks can be joined straight together, or on-point, to form a design, with or without sashing strips. Different blocks can be used in the same quilt. Strips may also be sewn log-cabin style around blocks before joining them together. You could also consider setting the quilt with plain squares in between the pieced squares, as these will break up the individual blocks and allow the quilting to enhance the design. Examples of nine different quilt settings are given for each of the fifteen blocks in this book.

Adding Sashing Strips

Some patterns look better if sashing strips are used to separate the blocks or groups of blocks. Ideally the sashing strips will be the same width as, or narrower than, the squares in the blocks. If using sashing to separate groups of blocks, piece these groups first and then treat them as a single unit.

Lay the blocks (or units) out in order, then sew a sashing strip to the right-hand side of each block except the one on the end of the row. Now sew the blocks into rows.

Stitch a sashing strip to the bottom of each row except the last and sew the rows together to complete the quilt.

Adding Borders

If you are adding a border, the width needs to be in proportion to the quilt blocks and to the sashing. You can have just one border or multiple borders. One narrow border with a wide, outer border can look effective.

QUILTING

Once the quilt top is pieced, it can be quilted in a number of different ways. Consider fine hand quilting, machine quilting, tie quilting or big stitch quilting.

Most quilts can be quilted by following the design of the quilt – quilting around the stars and around each block. An alternative is to ignore the quilt top pattern and impose a different quilting design on top. Curves, diagonal lines or a wave pattern all look effective. You could also quilt motifs at intervals on the quilt, in the central squares perhaps, or on plain units, particularly where these form a larger plain area in the quilt.

Tacking (Basting)

Cut the wadding (batting) and backing about 1in (2.5cm) larger all round than the quilt top. Press the backing and quilt top. Spread the backing out on a large flat surface, right side down. Fasten the backing down – with masking tape or pins if you are working on a carpet – so that it remains taut and wrinkle free while you tack (baste) the layers together. Place the wadding centrally on the backing and the quilt top, right side up, on top of the wadding. Pin with safety pins or tack the three layers together in a grid pattern to hold them together. Start from the centre and work out to the edges, smoothing out the wrinkles as you go.

Hand Quilting

You may like to put your work in a frame to help hold it fairly taut – but not drum tight. Start at the centre and 'pop' your knot so it disappears in the layers. Using a running stitch,

make sure you sew through all three layers by catching the needle on your finger underneath as you rock it back up. When at the end of your thread, or the line you are sewing, tie a knot and again 'pop' it through and lose it in the layers. The size of your stitches should be even. It takes practise, so don't expect prize-winning quilting at your first attempt.

Machine Quilting

It is best to start with a small practice piece first to ensure that your machine is set up correctly, using the same materials as for the quilt. Set the machine up for darning, if you are going to do free machining, otherwise, for straight stitch quilting fit the walking foot to your machine. You will probably need to loosen the top tension slightly and perhaps also tighten the bottom tension. This is to ensure that the stitch lies flat in the work and no loops of bottom thread show on the top.

Start with the stitch length set to virtually zero and gradually increase it to a fairly long stitch. Follow the quilting line as accurately as you can and finish by gradually decreasing the stitch length down to zero again. These tiny stitches are almost impossible to pull out and will be secure enough for a quilt that won't get much wear and tear. For a quilt that will be washed often, knot the thread ends 'pop' them in the wadding (batting) as you would for hand quilting.

Tie Quilting

This gives a puffy effect by fastening the three layers together at discreet intervals with a knotted thread. Use an embroidery or crochet thread and a large needle – you may find a curved needle is easier. Place the needle where you want the tie to be. Take one stitch through all three layers, leaving a long tail of thread at the beginning. Take another stitch in the same place, pull it tight, and cut off the thread, leaving a long tail. Tie the two tail threads together using a reef knot if possible, although a granny knot is acceptable.

Big Stitch Quilting

As its name implies this form of hand quilting does not involve doing the smallest stitch you can. Use a contrasting embroidery or crochet thread and stitch your design over the quilt using a neat running stitch. The stitches should be a sensible size – not toe catchers, but not twelve to the inch – and evenly spaced as they would be for fine hand quilting. You will find that the thickness of the thread, the size of the needle and the thickness of the quilt will dictate the size of stitch you can achieve. With this form of quilting you can create all-

over patterns or quilt contrasting motifs over your project. Try quilting circles over a very geometric design for an interesting effect.

BINDING AND FINISHING

To finish the quilt, cut two strips of binding fabric 2in (5cm) wide and the length of the two sides of the quilt. Fold them in half lengthways, wrong sides together, and press. Pin the binding strips to the two sides of the quilt, matching the raw edges and stitch ⅝in (1.5cm) away from the raw edges. Roll the folded edge to the back of the quilt, pin and slip stitch in place. Make sure the stitches do not go through to the front of the quilt.

Cut two more 2in (5cm) wide strips, this time about 1in (2.5cm) longer than the top and bottom. Fold in half and press as before. Pin in place along the top and bottom edges allowing 1in (2.5cm) to overlap at each end. Stitch in place ⅝in (1.5cm) from the raw edges. Once again, roll the folded edge over to the back of the quilt to pin and slip stitch in place. As you do so, fold the overlap of the binding to the back of the quilt to make a neat finished corner with no raw edges showing.

Finally, and most importantly, make a label for the back of the quilt, stating who made it and when. You can add other information if you wish.

EIGHT-POINTED STAR

This star design is also known as the Lemoyne (or Lemon) Star and sometimes as Diamond Star. The star, based on an octagon, takes its name from the LeMoyne brothers who founded New Orleans. In the North, the name was corrupted to Lemon Star as the brothers' annexation of territory for France made them unpopular.

The pattern is provided overleaf as a 4in square and constructing eight-pointed stars is described on page 25 of Techniques.
Nine colourway examples are also given overleaf. As you can see the diamonds can be coloured all the same or in alternate shadings. When several blocks are set together they form a completely new design that can be coloured independently of the block outlines and thus losing the star altogether.

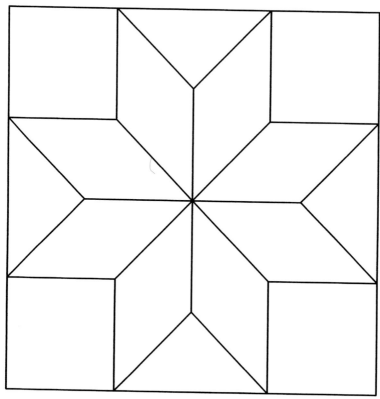

Colourways
Altering the colour of the corner squares can give a three-dimensional effect, as can colouring alternate diamonds the same shade as the triangles. The star can be coloured to lose the star design altogether.

Quilt Settings
In setting the block in quilts, try using mirror image colours in alternate blocks. The blocks can be set together, on point, or with sashing strips.

Block Pattern
This design is based on an octagon, in that the distance between each of the star points is equal. It is easiest and most accurate to hand piece this over papers. It can also be machine pieced, but take care over setting in the Y seams. Alternatively, the star itself can be pieced and then appliquéd to a background square.

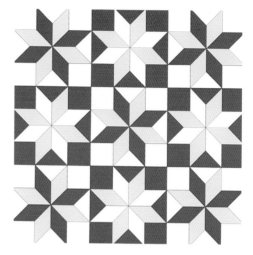

STAR OF THE EAST

This star is a variation of the Eight-pointed Star, being based on an octagon, with the diamonds split along the middle (see Techniques page 25 for constructing an eight-point star). The star looks best when the two halves of the diamonds are shaded dark and light to give a three-dimensional effect.

Experiment with different shadings to emphasise this quality and consider using more colours in the background to help create interest where blocks are set together. Instead of using two fabrics, look out for interesting striped fabrics for the star rays – this has the added advantage of reducing the number of seams meeting in the centre of this block, which perhaps makes it an unsuitable one for beginners.

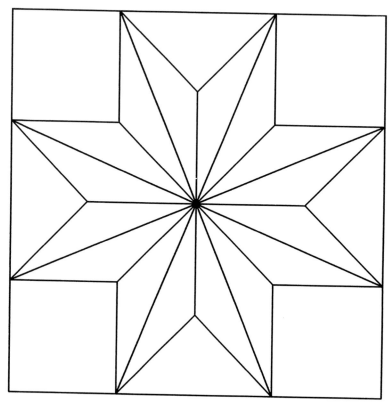

Colourways
Notice how changing the colour of the star and background alters the appearance of the block.

Quilt Settings
The block can be set with or without sashing strips and on point. Alternating the colour of the background can be effective, as can colouring the background to create a secondary pattern where blocks meet.

Block Pattern
This block is pieced in the same way as the Eight-pointed Star – piecing over papers (English piecing) is probably the most accurate method to use.

A quick way to piece the diamonds is to cut two strips of fabric, seam them together and cut the diamonds out from the stripped fabric, ensuring the seam line is along the centre.

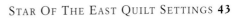

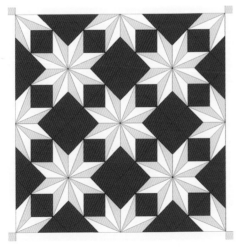

EMPIRE STAR

This eight-pointed star has unequal rays and a handy 'button' to hide the fact that the points don't always meet (this of course ensures that they will). Why not use this disguising technique on other stars – there is no rule that says you are not allowed to!

Constructing the block is straightforward enough (see Techniques page 25 for constructing an eight-pointed star), while imaginative colour choices yield some fascinating variations. You can see by the quilt settings on pages 48–9 that alternating plain quilted blocks with the pieced blocks is also effective. Notice too the effect of putting the star on a dark background.

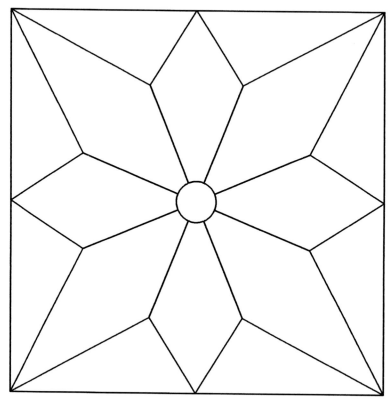

Colourways

The appliqué circle can be coloured to match the background or one set of star points. Although not shown here, the star points can all be the same colour.

Quilt Settings

The blocks can be set with or without sashings and on point. Notice how secondary circular and star patterns can appear where the long star rays intersect.

Block Pattern

This block has set-in seams and is probably most accurately pieced over papers. Take care with the background triangles if machine piecing. At least with this block, you don't have to panic when the seams don't meet in the centre, as the circle is neatly appliquéd over the join.

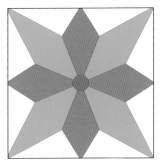
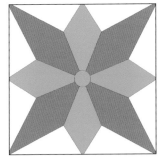
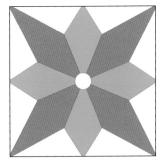
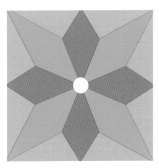
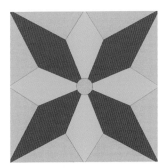

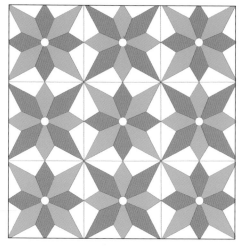
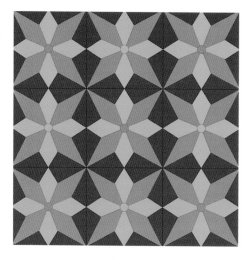
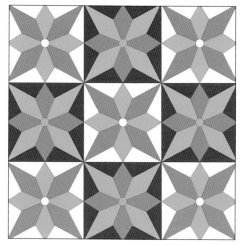

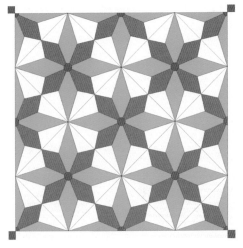

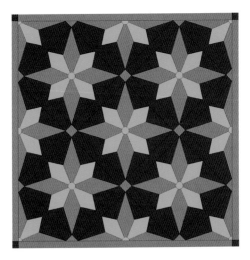

FRIENDSHIP STAR

This is a very simple block to make (see Techniques page 22 for constructing a nine-patch block). The central square can be left plain, to be embroidered with names when making a friendship quilt as a gift – hence its name.

The pattern can also be given an extra three-dimensional effect by using folded triangles for the star rays; these can be rolled back and slip stitched down to give a slight curve as well.

This is an excellent block for a beginner to gain confidence in machine or hand piecing and in the use of a rotary cutter. Different aspects of the block can be emphasised by colour placement – for instance, the star can be made to recede if alternate background squares are strongly coloured in comparison.

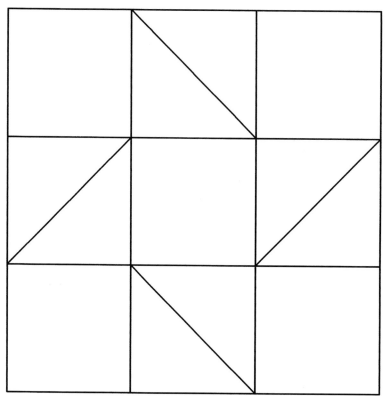

Colourways
The block lends itself to a bold colour scheme and it is very effective when set with other blocks.

Quilt Settings
The block can be set on point, straight, and with or without sashing. It can look very geometric when identical blocks are set together, but try colouring the entire quilt design, ignoring the boundaries of the block, and see what you come up with.

Block Pattern
This very simple nine-patch block is composed of squares and half-square triangles and can be easily machine pieced for quick results. More detailed piecing instructions and diagrams are given in Techniques page 22.

OHIO STAR

This block has a great number of names and variations – one of these is Variable Star. You may also come across this block as Aunt Eliza's Star, Lone Star or Texas Star. It dates back to the early 1880s, frequently occurs in tiled floor patterns and was a great favourite in larger Victorian houses for hallways and front door steps.

Ohio Star is a very popular block with quiltmakers as it is easy to make and looks very different each time you use it. It is also effective used with other blocks and as a miniature in the sashing and border corner blocks.

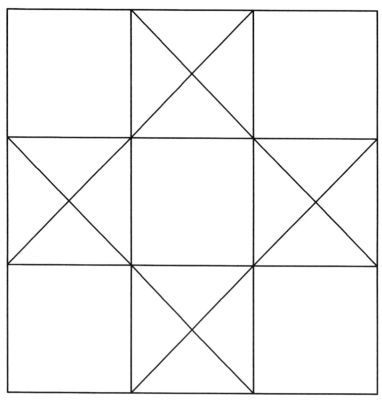

Colourways

Notice how altering the placement of colours can change the block quite radically, which is probably the reason it has so many names.

Quilt Settings

The block can be set straight or on point and with or without sashing. Alternating mirror image colours of blocks can be effective, using different sizes of block within one quilt – use the smaller ones as a border perhaps.

Block Pattern

This is a nine-patch block made from squares and quarter-square triangles, and is the one most often used to teach machine piecing of nine-patch. More detailed piecing instructions and diagrams are given in Techniques page 22.

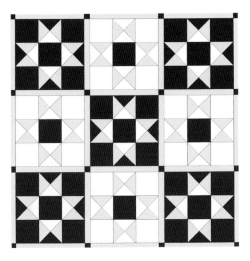

54-40 OR FIGHT

The unusual name for this block arose from the dispute over the boundary between the United States and Canada. '54-40 or Fight' was the rallying call used by supporters of James Polk, who won the US presidential election in 1844, and arose from a dispute between Great Britain and the United Statesover the Oregon boundary .
Polk's supporters wished the boundary to be set at 54° 40'. As President, James Polk settled the Oregon boundary dispute by establishing the 49th parallel as the US/Canadian border.

This is another interesting block that can be set straight and then coloured in a number of ways, including ignoring the block boundaries and losing the star pattern altogether. A quilt competition some years ago, based on nine of these blocks set together, produced a set of quilts in which it was very difficult to find the original blocks.

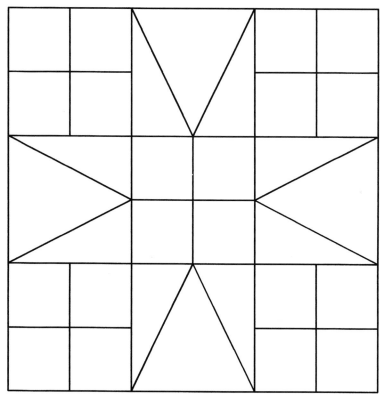

Colourways

As you can see, the four-patch squares march boldly across the block and quilts, and careful colouring of these can produce some interesting secondary patterns where the blocks meet.

Quilt Settings

The pictures on pages 66–7 show that the quilts can be set with or without sashing and with blocks straight or on point for a variety of very different looks.

Block Pattern

This nine-patch block is easily machine pieced. The four-patch squares can be quick pieced by sewing two strips (one of each colour), the width of each smaller square plus seam allowance, together and slicing them apart into strips – again the width of the squares. Sew these in pairs, alternating the colours, to produce four-patch squares quickly and easily.

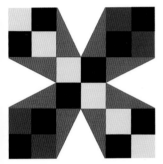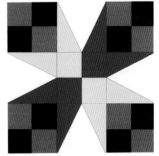

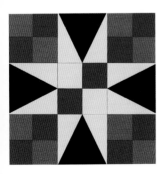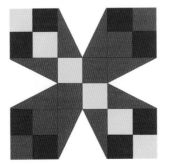

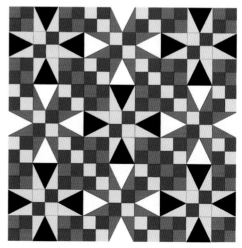

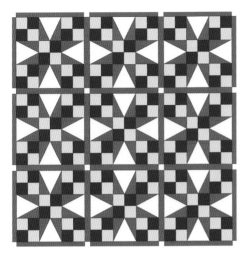

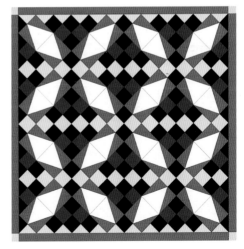

INDIAN STAR

This is a four-patch block, a variation of Sawtooth Star, which is identical to Indian Star but with a plain (unpieced) central square. 'Sawtooth' is the generic name given to blocks of this type.

Like the nine-patch 54-40 or Fight design, the squares march boldly across the block and the quilts but different colourings can disguise or alter this. The block can be set with similar four-patch variations of Sawtooth Star or with plain quilted squares.

Formed from squares and two types of triangle, you will see it sometimes with the background triangle split to form two right-angled triangles, but unless you are using a quick piecing method for half-square triangles, there is no real advantage in this.

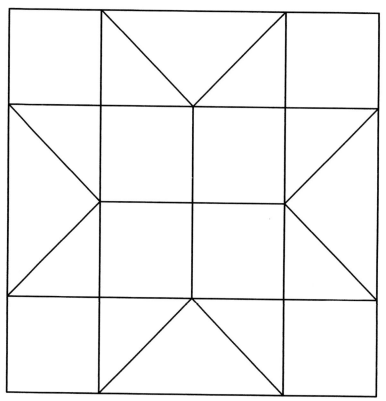

Colourways

Notice how the star can seem to disappear in some colourings. The block can be coloured to emphasise the star, or to lose it altogether. Other colourings can highlight the squares to set them marching across the quilt.

Quilt Settings

The quilts can be set with straight or on point blocks and with or without sashing. The sashing colour can be used to point up the star or to emphasise the squares even further.

Block Pattern

This simple four-patch block is made from squares and two types of triangle and is very easy to machine piece (see Techniques page 25 for constructing four-patch blocks).

SIMPLE STAR

This is also known as Lemoyne Star Variation. Like Lemoyne Star, this star is based on an octagon but because the set-in squares and triangles are split, the block can be pieced as a four-patch.

Lemoyne (or LeMoyne) Star takes its name from the LeMoyne brothers who founded New Orleans. The name was corrupted to Lemon Star in the North as the brothers became increasingly unpopular over their annexing of more territory for France.

The block is usually coloured using two strongly contrasting shades and can be shaded in a number of ways to lose the star completely.

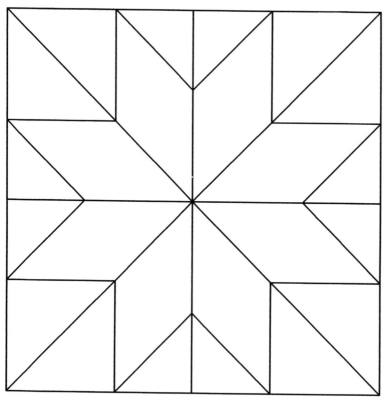

Colourways

This pattern looks very effective in two alternating, contrasting colours. The addition of a third colour increases the possibilities and the block can then be shaded in a number of ways to lose the star completely.

Quilt Settings

The block can be set straight or on point. Interesting secondary patterns appear at the intersection of the blocks so it is worth setting it without sashing. This is another design that lends itself to being coloured without regard to the block boundaries.

Block Pattern

Although an eight-pointed star, this can be machine pieced as a four-patch block. There are a considerable number of seams meeting in the centre so take care here – it may be worth stitching the last seam from the centre out. Careful pressing of the seam allowances will also help to minimise any bulk.

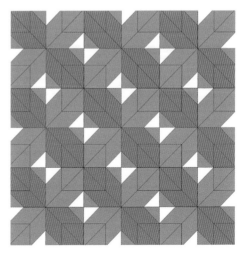

BLAZING STAR

This block is just one of a number of designs called Blazing Star. This is a common problem in naming quilt designs; there are many different blocks with the same name, or alternatively, there are many names for one design – such as Ohio Star.

This Blazing Star is a four-patch block with the two halves being mirror images of each other. It is a simple but elegant star that can be coloured to give the appearance of two very different stars superimposed, or the same star with the upper one rotated, as you can see by the nine colourways shown overleaf. The split rays are best coloured in two shades to give a three-dimensional effect.

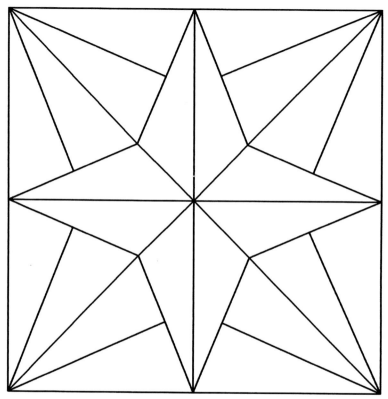

Colourways
Notice the difference a dark background can make to the appearance of both the block and the quilts.

Quilt Settings
When the blocks are set without sashing, secondary star patterns are formed at block intersections and seem especially noticeable when the blocks are on point.

Block Pattern
Details of piecing a four-patch block are given in Techniques page 25. Take care at the centre where eight seams meet – it may be easier to seam from the centre out. The two halves of the rays can be speed pieced, or cut from striped fabric to reduce the total number of centre seams.

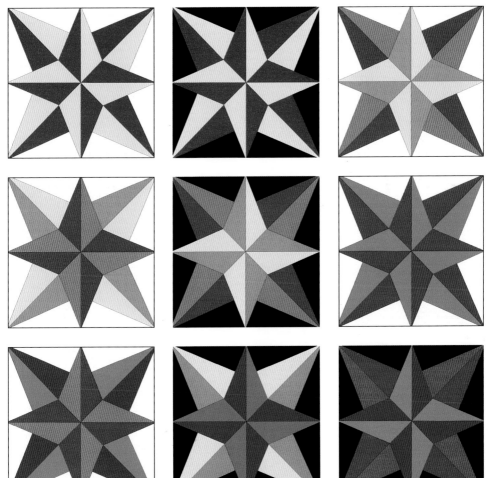

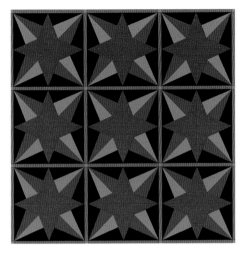

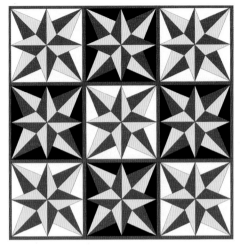

EVENING STAR

This star is a variation of an eight-pointed star and is based on an octagon. The block can be pieced by machine or by hand and is composed of eight large triangles each subdivided into four smaller ones.

The central ring of triangles can be coloured alternately, or you can use a transparent template, as described in Techniques page 20, to cut eight identical motifs from your fabric to create a kaleidoscope effect in the centre. This is particularly effective in larger blocks used alone, with a border of the same fabric perhaps, in cushions or wall hangings.

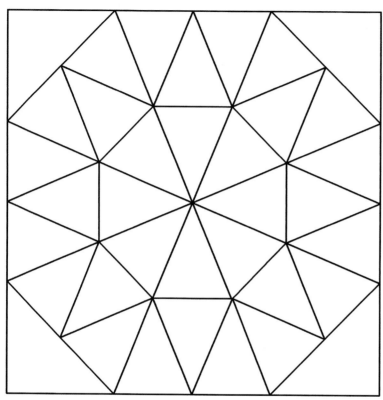

Colourways

The colours can be placed to emphasise different parts of the block – the eight-pointed star or the four-pointed star for instance. The circular illusion of the block, most noticeable when blocks are set together, can also be highlighted.

Quilt Settings

As with all the star blocks, these can be set straight or on point and with or without sashing; other eight-pointed stars can be used in conjunction with it. Different colourings can emphasise many secondary patterns where blocks intersect.

Block Pattern

This variation of an eight-pointed star can be pieced by machine or by hand and is composed of eight large triangles each subdivided into four smaller ones. Each large triangle is pieced first, then the eight triangles are sewn together. Finally add the corner triangles to complete the square. Take care at the centre where so many seam lines meet to ensure a neat finish to the block.

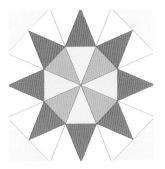

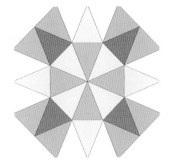
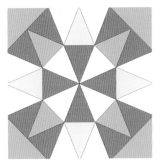
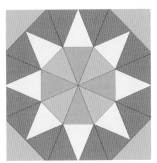
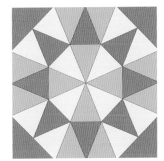
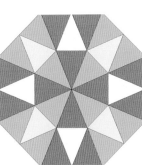
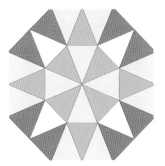
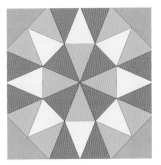

SKYROCKET

This block has a miniature nine-patch in the centre, though there are a number of similar blocks where the central star is larger or more complicated. The colouring of the block can emphasise different aspects of the pattern – the star at the centre or the star rays (or rockets) at the corners.

The quilt settings on pages 96–7 show that the rays form secondary patterns where the blocks meet. Putting the block on point emphasises the central star block. This block also looks effective when set with a similar block – in this case Empire Star on page 44. Four blocks can be straight set to form a centre medallion, with a contrast colourway used to create the illusion of a border. Note also the effect of having two colours in the background.

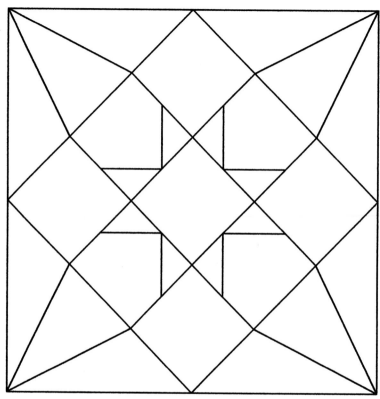

Colourways

As you can see by the nine variations, the colouring chosen for the skyrocket block can emphasise different aspects – the star at the centre or the star rays (rockets) at the corners.

Quilt Settings

Note how different coloured backgrounds can affect the look of the quilt and create secondary patterns. This block also looks effective when set with plain quilted blocks.

Block Pattern

This is a fairly easy block, which can be either machine or hand pieced. The 4in block shown here has a miniature nine-patch in the centre. Piece the nine-patch first, then the corner triangles, adding them to the centre block.

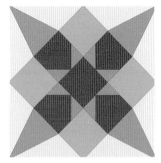

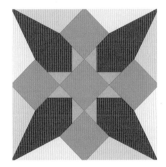
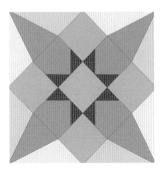
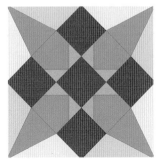

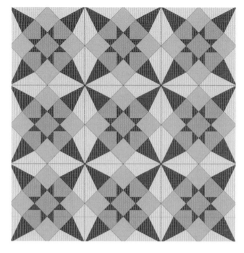

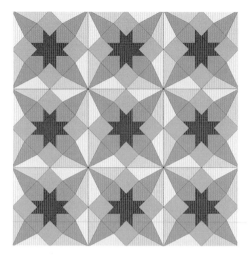

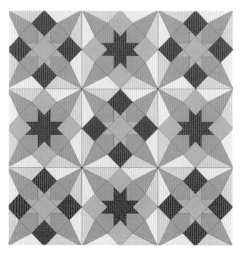

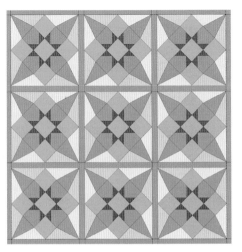

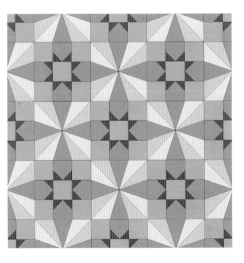

INTERLACED STAR

This diagonally pieced four-patch block is composed of four triangles rather than four squares. It can be coloured in two ways – to make it look as if the star rays are interlaced (hence its name), or to give the appearance of one star superimposed on another. It also makes a good corner block for borders and sashings – as do many star blocks.

The design is of fairly recent origin compared with traditional designs such as Ohio Star. It could be fun to add some extra seam lines so that the star rays can be coloured to give a transparent effect where they weave under and over each other.

Colourways
The rays can be different shades of the same colour, two colours or even four contrasting colours. In addition, note the difference a dark background can make.

Quilt Settings
When set into a quilt, the block works well whether set on point or straight and with or without sashing.

Block Pattern
First piece the background triangles and smaller interlaced triangle. Sew this to the longer interlaced star ray to complete each large triangle (see constructing four-patch stars in Techniques page 25) and finally sew the four triangles together.

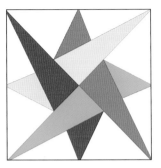
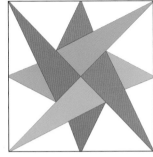

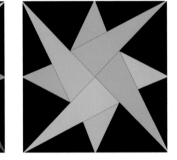

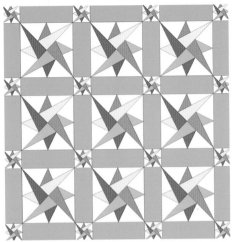

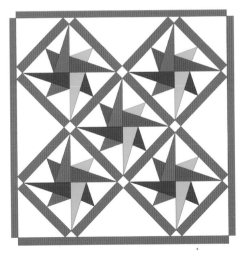

TWISTED STAR

This variation of an eight-pointed star is based on an octagon and has a partial seam (see Techniques page 28 for constructing a star with a partial seam). It is far simpler to create than it looks. Along with many of the star patterns in this book this star can be pieced as a scrap quilt. Try using different fabrics of the same colour (for example, all green or all blue) for the star rays.

Do experiment with different colourings and quilt settings and try using it in conjunction with other eight-pointed stars, perhaps the Eight-pointed Star, page 32, made with a striped fabric, or with plain quilted blocks. Try also using the block on point as a border to a quilt, or as corner blocks.

Colourways

The block lends itself to dramatic colours or prints but can also look very effective in softer shades. Experiment with stripes and checks too; these can be used to great effect in many star patterns.

Quilt Settings

Like so many of the star blocks it can appear very geometric in a straight set, but when a little variety of colour is added, secondary patterns start to become visible.

Block Pattern

This block can be stitched by hand or machine and contains a partial seam. The first triangle is stitched to the octagon, but only half the seam is sewn. The other triangles and squares can then be added in rotation. The final, partial, seam is then completed.

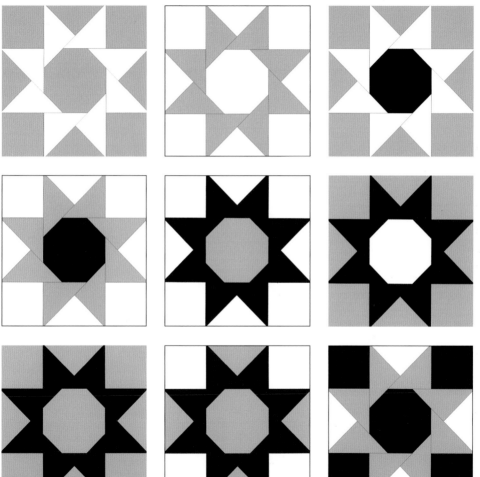

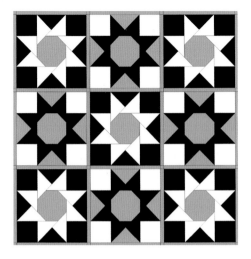

ECCENTRIC STAR

This is an interesting star formation with a simple square within a square block at its centre and a strong pattern of radiating rays. It is another block with a partial seam that, again, looks more complicated to piece than it actually is.

The quilt settings on pages 114-15 show some of the possible variations. The pattern can be used in conjunction with plain quilted blocks, as a corner block, or set with other similar stars. As its rays go to the corner of the block it would look best set with blocks such as Spinning Stars, Blazing Star or Skyrocket, although my favourite would be Interlaced Star, page 98.

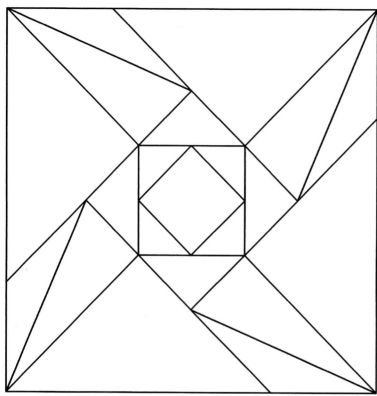

Colourways
Different colourings emphasise different parts of the star rays and add to the whirling effect created when blocks are put together.

Quilt Settings
This block can be set on point, straight, and with or without sashing strips. Note how different the block appears when placed on point and how a strongly contrasting background can enhance the finished pattern.

Block Pattern
The central square within a square block is pieced first. The star rays are pieced and added to the background triangles. Finally these triangles are stitched around the central square. The first seam is a partial seam (stitched only part way), the other triangles can then be added in rotation and the final seam completed.

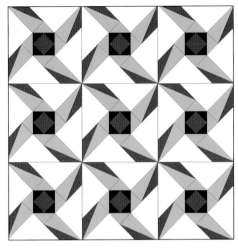

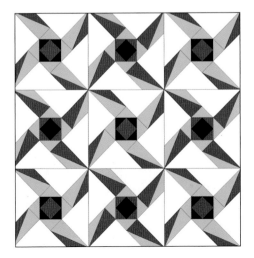

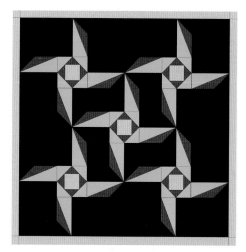

SPINNING STARS

This is a wonderful block which makes up into some very different quilts. There are two four-pointed stars superimposed on each other and the colouring can emphasise this. The four-pointed star of half-square triangles resembles the Friendship Star block and is superimposed on another block known as World Without End or The Priscilla.

It is perhaps not a suitable block for a beginner as its construction includes a partial seam, but it is worth trying once you have mastered the basics of patchwork. The block also works well as a quilting pattern in plain setting blocks.

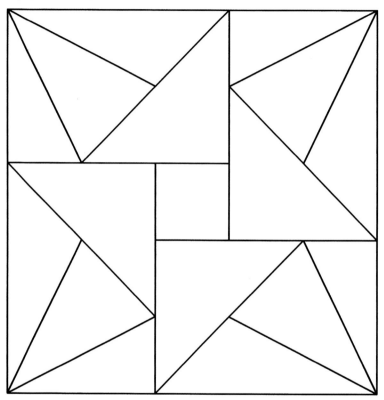

Colourways

The block can be coloured in a number of ways to emphasise the two superimposed stars and to create interesting effects in the background when blocks are set together.

The central square could be coloured to give a transparent effect from the two superimposed patterns – e.g. a red and yellow star, resulting in an orange central square.

Quilt Settings

When the blocks are put together the different colourings can create some eye-catching secondary patterns.

Block Pattern

This is another block with a partial seam and is stitched from the outside to the centre. Piece the outer star rays and background triangles first then sew these to the inner star ray triangles. Finally sew them to the centre square: the first seam will be a partial one; then add the other triangles in rotation and finally complete the first seam.

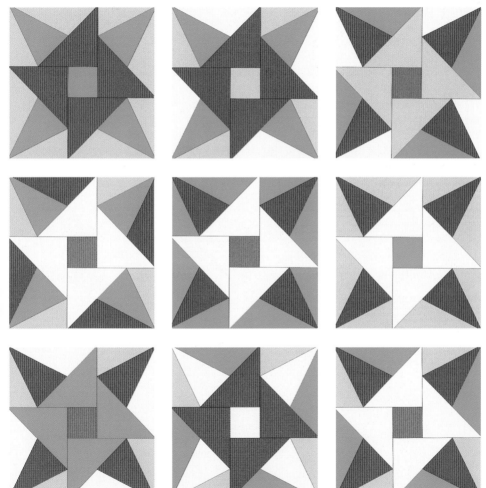

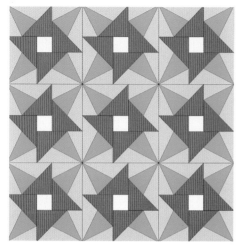

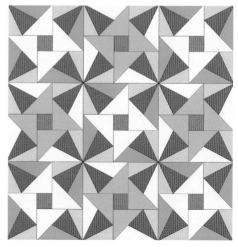

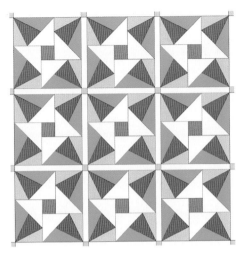

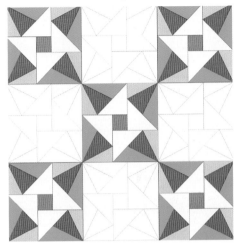

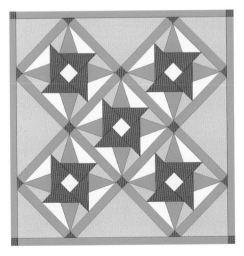

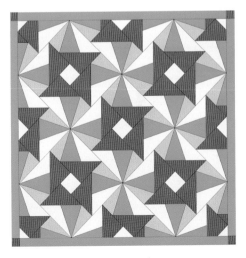

FURTHER VARIATIONS

As you can see, there is a whole host of variations on the star pattern. I have given details of some the more traditional, or interesting ones, but there are plenty of variations on these basic patterns that you can discover yourself simply by adding lines to or subtracting lines from the initial block. Here are a few examples to start you off on your star quest. The block patterns shown can be changed to whatever size you like using either graph paper or a photocopier.

Swamp Angel

Judy in Arabia

Blazing Star Variation

Six-pointed Star

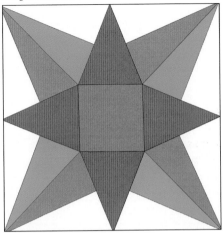

Barbara Frietchie Star

St Louis Star

Texas Star

Feathered Star

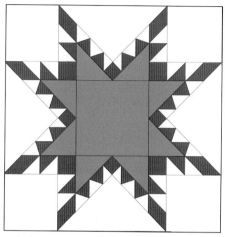

Optical Illusions

Whirling Star

Rolling Star

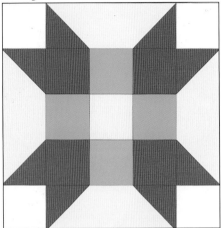

Missouri Star

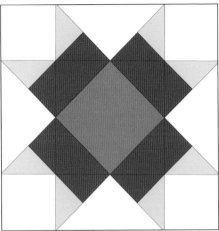

St Louis Star

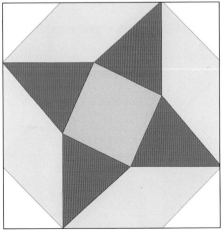

Hunter's Star

Guiding Star

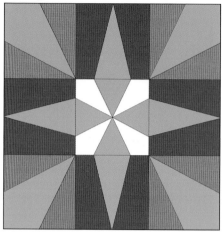

Square and Stars

Western Star

Morning Star

BIBLIOGRAPHY

This is not intended as a comprehensive list of books, but rather an indication of some you may find useful.

Anderson, Alex, *Simply Stars – Quilts That Sparkle* (C&T Publishing, 1996)

Beyer, Jinny, *The Quilter's Album of Blocks and Borders* (Bell & Hyman, 1980)

Chainey, Barbara, *The Essential Quilter* (David & Charles, 1993)

Chainey, Barbara, *Quilt It!* (David & Charles, 1998)

Hargrave, H., *Heirloom Machine Quilting* (C&T Publishing, Revised ed. 1990)

Hargrave, H., and Craig, S., *The Art of Classic Quiltmaking* (C&T Publishing, 1999)

Johnson, M. E., *Star Quilts* (Quilt Digest Press, 1996)

La Branche, Carol, *A Constellation for Quilters* (The Main Street Press, 1986)

Martin, Judy, *Shining Star Quilts* (Moon Over the Mountain Publ. Co., 1987)

McCloskey, Marsha, *Feathered Star Sampler* (That Patchwork Place, 1985)

McCloskey, Marsha, *Feathered Star Quilts* (That Patchwork Place, 1987)

McCloskey, M., and Martin, N., *Variable Star Quilts* (Dover Publications, 1995)

Meunier, C., *Easy Traditional Quilts: Stars* (Chitra Publications, 1999)

Reis, Sherry, *Eight-pointed Stars* (That Patchwork Place, 1999)

Reynolds, B. S., *Stars à la carte* (American Quilter's Society, 1999)

Searl, G., *Sew Many Stars: Techniques and Patterns* (American Quilt Society, 1998)

Seward, Linda, *Patchwork, Appliqué and Quilting* (Mitchell Beazley, Revised ed. 1996)

Thomas, D. L., *Shortcuts: a Concise Guide to Rotary Cutting* (That Patchwork Place, 1991)

Williamson, Darra Duffy, *Stars: Classic American Quilt Collection* (Rodale Press, 1997)

INDEX

ACKNOWLEDGEMENTS

With many thanks to Barbara, who started it all. To Arnot and Rebecca (who helped design the quilts) for putting up with the more than usual haphazard domestic engineering, and for sorting out problems with the computer. To Patricia Cox for allowing access to, and photographs of, her wonderful collection of quilts; and to members of the Quilters' Guild of the British Isles and Staffordshire Patchworkers for their friendship, help and advice. The blocks and quilts were drawn with the aid of the Electric Quilt computer program EQ4, supplied by Rio Designs; thanks also to Lawrence Dawes of Rio for his help.